THE JUNGLE BOOK

BY RUDYARD KIPLING

Abridged and adapted by Anne L. Nelan

Illustrated by Earl Thollander

A PACEMAKER CLASSIC

FEARON/JANUS
Belmont, California

Simon & Schuster Supplementary Education Group

Other Pacemaker Classics

The Adventures of Huckleberry Finn
The Adventures of Tom Sawyer
A Christmas Carol
Crime and Punishment
The Deerslayer
Dr. Jekyll and Mr. Hyde
Ethan Frome
Frankenstein
Great Expectations
Jane Eyre
The Last of the Mohicans
Moby Dick
The Moonstone
The Red Badge of Courage
Robinson Crusoe
The Scarlet Letter
A Tale of Two Cities
The Three Musketeers
The Time Machine
Treasure Island
20,000 Leagues Under the Sea
Two Years Before the Mast
Wuthering Heights

Library of Congress Catalog Card Number: 67-25785

ISBN 0–8224–9210–5

Printed in the United States of America

CONTENTS

Mowgli's Mother

Mowgli

Shere Khan

Baloo

Kaa

Bagheera

1 MOWGLI'S BROTHERS

It was a very warm night in the Seeonee Hills of India. Father Wolf woke up from his day's rest. Mother Wolf lay with her big gray nose dropped across her four sleeping cubs.

"I must get up," said Father Wolf. "It is time to hunt again."

But before he could leave his cave, he heard a cry from the Jungle. It was the cry of a tiger —Shere Khan. But it was the cry of a tiger who has caught nothing. And Shere Khan did not care if all the Jungle heard him.

"Bad!" said Father Wolf. "To begin a night's work with that noise! Does Shere Khan think the deer of the Jungle have no ears?"

"It is not deer that he is hunting," said Mother Wolf. "It is Man."

"Man!" said Father Wolf, showing all his white teeth. "And on our ground too!"

The Law of the Jungle says the animals must not hunt man. If one man is killed by an animal, other men will come to the Jungle. The men will hunt and kill the animals. They will drive them from their homes.

Shere Khan roared. It was the cry he made when jumping for his kill. Then he gave another cry. This cry sounded more like a kitten.

"He has missed," said Mother Wolf. "Listen! Something is coming up the hill. Get ready."

A noise came from behind a rock. Father Wolf pulled his legs under him, ready to jump. Then, had you been looking, you would have seen a strange thing. Father Wolf jumped before he saw what he was jumping at. He flew straight up in the air for about five feet. Then he tried to stop himself. He landed almost at the same spot where he left the ground.

"Man!" he barked. "A man's cub. Look!"

There stood a brown baby without any clothes on. He was as soft and sweet a thing as ever came into a wolf's cave. He looked up into Father Wolf's face and laughed.

"Is that a man's cub?" asked Mother Wolf. "I have never seen one. Bring it here. Put it next to our cubs."

A wolf moves its own cubs by holding them in its mouth. Father Wolf's mouth closed right on the baby's back. But his teeth did not hurt the baby. And he laid him down with the cubs.

"How little!" said Mother Wolf. "And he has no hair on him. So this is a man's cub. Now was there ever a wolf that took care of a man's cub?"

"I have heard now and again of such a thing," answered Father Wolf. "But I have never seen it."

"I could kill him with my foot," said Mother Wolf. "But see! He looks up and is not afraid."

Just then, Shere Khan's great head pushed into the mouth of the cave. "Where is my meat?" he asked. "A man's cub went this way. Its mother and father have run off. Give it to me."

Shere Khan was very angry because he was hungry. But Father Wolf was not afraid. He knew that the mouth of the cave was too small for Shere Khan. The tiger could only get his head inside the cave.

"Wolves don't do what tigers tell them to do," said Father Wolf. "We listen only to the Head of the Pack. The man-cub is ours—to kill if we want to."

"What talk is this? It is I, Shere Khan, who tells you." The tiger's roar filled the cave.

Mother Wolf left her cubs and jumped to the mouth of the cave. She faced the hungry eyes of Shere Khan.

"And it is I, Mother Wolf, who answers," she said. "The man-cub belongs to me. He shall not be killed. He shall live to run with the Wolf Pack. He shall hunt with the Pack. In the end he shall hunt *you!* Now go!"

Shere Khan backed away. "We shall see what the Wolf Pack says about this," he roared. "The man-cub belongs to me. He will come to my teeth in the end."

Mother Wolf threw herself down next to the cubs.

"Shere Khan is right in that," Father Wolf said. "The Wolf Pack may not want this man-cub. Will you still keep him, Mother?"

"He came to us alone. But he was not afraid!" cried Mother Wolf. "And Shere Khan would kill him. Keep him? Yes, I will keep him. I will call him Mowgli, for he looks like a little frog."

As soon as wolf cubs can stand alone, their fathers must show them to the Pack. That way, every wolf knows who belongs to the Pack. It is the Law of the Jungle.

Father Wolf waited until his four cubs could walk a little. Then he took them and Mowgli and Mother Wolf to the Council Rock. The Council Rock was the top of the hill where the Wolf Pack met. Akela, Head of the Pack, lay on his rock. He was a big gray wolf. About 40 wolves lay around him.

There was little talking at the Council Rock. The cubs were playing. Their mothers and fathers sat watching them. Now and again, an old wolf would go up to a cub. He would look him over. Then he would go back to his place.

"You know the Law!" cried Akela. "Look well, oh wolves. These now are wolves of the Pack."

Then Father Wolf pushed Mowgli in front of the Pack. An angry roar went up. Shere Khan's voice came from behind the Council Rock. "The man-cub is my meat. Give him to me."

"Yes," said a young wolf, showing his teeth. "What have we to do with a man-cub? Give him to Shere Khan."

One wolf had said Mowgli should not be in the Pack. Now two must say they want him in the Pack. And these two can not be his mother or father. If two did not say they want him, Mowgli would go to Shere Khan. That is the Law of the Jungle.

"Who wants the man-cub?" asked Akela.

At first, there was no answer. Then Baloo, the brown bear, stood up. Even though he was not a wolf, he belonged to the Pack. He taught the wolf cubs the Law of the Jungle. "The man-cub will not hurt us," he said. "I will teach him."

"We need still another," said Akela.

Bagheera, the black panther, walked over to Mowgli. All the wolves knew Bagheera. And they were all afraid of him.

"Oh Akela, and you, wolves of the Pack," Bagheera said. "I have no right to stand up for the man-cub. I do not belong to the Wolf Pack. But one can pay the Pack to keep a cub. Does not the Law of the Jungle say that?"

"Good! Good!" cried the young wolves, who were always hungry. "Listen to Bagheera. Let him pay us."

"Keep the man-cub," said Bagheera, "and I will give a fat deer. Will you do it?"

There was the sound of many wolves howling. "Let us keep him!" was the cry.

Shere Khan gave an angry roar. He knew now that he would not get to eat Mowgli that night.

"Take the man-cub away," said Akela to Father Wolf. "Bring him up as one of the Wolf Pack."

2 KAA'S HUNTING

Day after day, Baloo taught Mowgli the Law of the Jungle. Wolves learn only as much of the Law as they need. But Mowgli, being a man-cub, had to learn much more. He soon grew tired of learning so much.

"Think how small he is," said Bagheera to Baloo. Bagheera had come to see how Mowgli was getting along. He sat rubbing his black head on Mowgli's leg. "How can his little head carry all your long talk?"

"He is so little he might get killed!" cried Baloo. "That is why I teach him these things. I am now teaching him the Master Words of the Jungle."

"What Master Words?" asked Bagheera.

"Mowgli," said Baloo, "show Bagheera what I have taught you."

"We be of one blood, you and I," said Mowgli. These were the Master Words for the Hunting People. Mowgli liked to show off. He made a face at Baloo.

"But," Mowgli said to Bagheera, "I know the Master Words of *all* the Jungle People. He

9

climbed on Bagheera's strong back. "Soon I shall have a Pack of my own. Did you know that? They will follow me high up in the trees all day long."

"They?" said Baloo in an angry voice. "Have you been talking with the Monkey People?"

"Why not!" said Mowgli. "They gave me fruits and nuts to eat. They took me in their arms up to the very tops of the trees. If I had a tail, I would look just like them. They said one day I would be Head of the Monkey People."

"Listen, man-cub!" roared Baloo. "The Monkey People have no Head. They have no Law. They talk a lot, but they do nothing. The falling of a nut turns their thoughts. We of the Jungle have nothing to do with them. We do not drink where the monkeys drink. We do not go where the monkeys go. We do not hunt where they hunt. We do not even talk about them. Have you ever heard me talk about the Monkey People before?"

Mowgli felt as if all the Jungle were watching him. "No," he said in a little voice.

Just then, nuts and branches fell all around them. They could hear the Monkey People in the trees above them. The Monkey People had heard what Baloo said and were very angry. So, they threw nuts and branches down trying to hit him.

They followed Baloo, Bagheera, and Mowgli as they went through the Jungle.

Soon it was time for the afternoon rest. Baloo and Bagheera lay down on the ground. Mowgli lay between them. In a few minutes, the three of them were sound asleep.

The next thing Mowgli knew, little paws had hold of his arms and legs. It was the Monkey People! They were carrying him up into the trees. Then branches hit his face. He looked down in time to see Bagheera jump up with an angry roar. The panther ran to the trunk of a tree. But he could not climb up high enough.

The monkeys laughed. "Bagheera can not come after us," they cried. "Only the Monkey People can climb high in the trees. We are a great people."

The monkeys were swinging from branch to branch far above the ground. Mowgli was afraid they would drop him. They were going very fast. His friends had been left far behind. He tried to think. He had to get word back to Bagheera and Baloo.

Just then, Mowgli saw Chil, the kite. Chil was flying through the blue sky looking for food.

Mowgli called the Master Words in kite talk. "We be of one blood, you and I," he called.

Then branches covered Mowgli. But Chil
followed him. When Mowgli could see Chil again,
he called in a loud voice, "Help! Tell Baloo which
way the monkeys are taking me."

"Who are you, Brother?" asked Chil. He had
heard of a man-cub in the Jungle. But he had
never seen Mowgli.

"I am Mowgli the Frog. They call me man-cub.
Tell Baloo!"

Baloo and Bagheera watched until they could not see Mowgli and the monkeys any more. They wanted to follow him, but were afraid to. "They will drop him if we follow too close," said Bagheera. "We must think of a plan."

"I have it!" cried Baloo. "The Monkey People fear only one animal—Kaa, the rock snake. He climbs as well as they do. He kills their young monkeys in the night. Just his name makes them afraid. Let us get Kaa."

Off they hurried to look for Kaa. They found him resting on a big rock. His yellow skin was shining in the sun.

"Good hunting!" said Baloo, as he came up to Kaa.

Like all snakes, Kaa did not hear well. He pulled back his head, ready to fight. Then he saw who it was.

"Good hunting for all of us," he answered. "What brings you two here? Do you know of any game near by? A deer? A young monkey?"

"We are hunting now," said Baloo.

"Let me come with you," said Kaa. "I am very hungry. I wait in a tree for days for something to eat to come along. And then, I don't always catch it. I came very near to falling on my last hunt," Kaa went on. "My tail lost its hold on the tree. I made such a noise that the Monkey People came to see what happened. They laughed and called me names."

"Big yellow worm!" said Bagheera, with a shake of his head.

"Did they call me that?" cried Kaa.

Bagheera smiled to himself. "They told me you are old and weak. They even said you have lost all your teeth. But who listens to the Monkey People?"

"It—it is the Monkey People we follow now," said Baloo. It was hard for him to say this, even to save Mowgli. No one in the Jungle ever talked about the Monkey People.

Kaa was surprised. "Why are you after the Monkey People?" he asked.

"Kaa, the monkeys took our man-cub," said Bagheera.

Kaa closed his eyes. "That is bad. A man-cub in their hands will get hurt. They grow tired of the nuts they pick. They throw them to the ground again. They may do the same with the man-cub.... They called me 'yellow fish,' was it not?"

"Worm, yellow worm," said Bagheera, "and other things too bad to say."

"They should watch what they say," said Kaa. "Their words make me very angry." Then he

looked up at the trees. "Now, where did they take your man-cub?"

"I know," came a cry. "Up! Baloo. Look up!"

Baloo looked up to see where the voice came from. He saw Chil, the kite, flying above them.

"I have followed Mowgli and the Monkey People," called Chil. "They took him to the monkey city, the Cold Lairs. First they showed him around the city. Then they left him alone and began to play.

"I saw Mowgli try to get away. He ran out of the Cold Lairs and almost got to the river. But then a monkey saw him and called to the others. They all went running after Mowgli. They caught him and took him back to the city. Then they shut him up in a room in one of the old buildings."

"Thank you, Chil," said Bagheera. "You are the best of kites."

"It is nothing," said Chil. "I had to follow him. The man-cub said the Master Words." Then Chil flew off through the sky.

The Cold Lairs was once a city full of people. Now there were no people in the great houses and the tall buildings. Grass and trees grew in the streets. All the people had left the city. No one knew why. Now, the Monkey People live there some of the time.

"Come, we must hurry to the Cold Lairs to find Mowgli," said Bagheera.

Bagheera ran as fast as he could toward the Cold Lairs. Kaa moved like a river over the ground. Poor Baloo was so slow he was soon left far behind.

"There is nothing slow about you," said Bagheera to Kaa.

"I am hungry," Kaa told him. "And I am angry. They called me a yellow frog."

"Worm," said Bagheera. "They called you a yellow worm."

"It is all the same to me," said Kaa.

"I wish Baloo were here," said Bagheera as they came to the Cold Lairs. "But we must do what we can without him. I will go in this way, Kaa. You go in from the other side. That way, we will surprise them."

Bagheera ran in and jumped the first monkey he saw. The monkey cried out. Other monkeys heard the cry and came running to help. All at once Bagheera was covered with monkeys. He could not fight them all at the same time. They bit him and pulled him down. He could see his own blood on the ground. They will kill me, Bagheera thought.

Then from the Jungle came the angry cry of Baloo. The old bear ran to help Bagheera as fast as he could. Baloo had come just in time! He stood up on his back legs and began to hit the monkeys. Blows from his paws threw the monkeys to the ground.

Then Kaa came from the other side of the Cold Lairs. He came straight for the monkeys. But he did not even need to fight. The Monkey People saw him and they were afraid.

"It is Kaa!" cried the monkeys. "Kaa! Run! Run!" All of the monkeys ran for the trees.

17

"Find the man-cub!" cried Bagheera. "I must rest." The great panther rested his head on his paws.

"Where is the man-cub?" asked Kaa.

Mowgli had heard all the noise. Now he cried out. "Here! I can not get out."

Kaa and Baloo followed the sound of Mowgli's voice. At last they found the right building and then the room. Kaa hit the door with his head again and again. The door fell in with a bang and Mowgli ran out.

"Are you hurt?" asked Baloo.

"A little," said Mowgli, throwing his arms around Baloo. "But not as much as you, my Brother."

"This is Kaa," said Baloo. "He saved our lives. Give him thanks."

Mowgli looked at the snake. "My kill is your kill, Kaa," said Mowgli. "When you are hungry, come to me. I will drive goats for you." Then he held out his hand to the snake.

Kaa put his head on the man-cub's hand. He was pleased. "That was well said," answered Kaa. "But now you must go. What follows is not for you to see."

Mowgli and Baloo went to find Bagheera. By this time the panther was feeling better. The three of them turned to watch Kaa.

Kaa looked at the monkeys. The monkeys were afraid and cried out.

"Can you see me?" Kaa asked, sliding over the ground.

"We see you, Kaa," the monkeys answered.

"Good!" said Kaa. "Now begins the dance, the Dance of the Kill of Kaa."

Kaa's head moved from left to right. He began winding around and around. He never stopped or rested. He sang as he moved. He was putting a spell on the monkeys. Watching Kaa made the eyes feel funny. He became one long, slow-moving wheel.

"Monkey People," said Kaa. "Will you do what I say?"

"Yes, great Kaa," the monkeys cried.

"Good!" Kaa said. "Take one step toward me."

The monkeys tried to stay where they were. But they could not. They had to take the step. Baloo and Bagheera took the step toward Kaa, too!

"Take another step," said Kaa. They all moved again.

Mowgli put his hands on Baloo and Bagheera. They jumped as if they had been asleep.

"Come away," said Mowgli.

"I am under Kaa's spell. Keep your hand on my head," said Bagheera. "If not, I must go back to Kaa."

The three of them ran off into the Jungle. They stopped to rest under some trees. Baloo and Bagheera were shaking.

"Never," said Baloo, "never will I hunt with Kaa again. I was under his spell. I would have walked right into his mouth!"

"He knows more than we," said Bagheera. "I, too, would have walked right into his mouth."

"But what was happening?" asked Mowgli. "I was not under Kaa's spell. I saw no more than a big snake playing games. And his nose was hurt," Mowgli laughed.

Bagheera grew angry when he heard Mowgli laughing at Kaa. "Mowgli, Kaa hurt his nose to save you. And Baloo and I are hurt, too. We will not be able to hunt for many days. All of this happened because you played with the Monkey People."

"You are right," said Mowgli. "I was bad. I will never play with the Monkey People again."

"Now," said Bagheera, "jump on my back, Little Brother. We are going home."

3 HOW FEAR CAME

In the winter, no rain fell. Spring came, but it was so dry the flowers did not grow. The sun pressed upon the Jungle. Little by little, the sun turned the leaves yellow. Still there was no rain. The sun was so hot that it turned everything brown and then black. The Jungle water holes turned first to mud. Hot winds blew. And then even the mud holes dried up.

The animals were all skin and bones. There was not enough food to eat. And there was very little water to drink. Bagheera killed three animals a day for food. Still he was hungry because the animals he killed were so thin. Not having enough water hurt the animals even more than not having enough food.

Day after day, Hathi, the elephant, watched the river go down. The river became small and slow. It was almost dried up. There came a time when he could walk across it. Then Hathi called for the Water Truce.

The Water Truce is a part of the Law of the Jungle. There is a Water Truce only when the rivers are almost dry. When the Water Truce is called, there can be no hunting by the river. All of the animals can come to the river to drink. They need not be afraid of being killed. Even tigers and deer drink together.

Chil, the kite, flew across the Jungle to tell all of the animals. "The Water Truce! The Water Truce is upon us," he called.

One afternoon, Bagheera and Mowgli stood by the river talking. Bagheera needed food. But he needed water even more. Up the river, many deer were standing by the water. Down the river were the wild pigs. Bagheera looked at all the animals he had once killed for food. Then he turned to Mowgli. "But for the Water Truce," he said. "It would be very good hunting."

Hathi, the elephant, stood near them. He heard Bagheera and answered him. "The Water Truce holds, Bagheera," he said. "This is no time to talk of hunting."

"Who knows better than I?" said Bagheera, rolling his yellow eyes. "For supper I had a frog."

Baloo came up to them. The old brown bear was shaking his head. "The river keeps going down. Oh Hathi," he asked, "have you ever seen anything like this before?"

"It will end. It will end," said Hathi. He blew water over his back with his trunk.

23

Just then, a roar came from the Jungle. It was Shere Khan. He was coming toward the river. He stopped when he saw Mowgli. "Must I see the man-cub every place I go?" he asked. "Next, I shall have to ask him if I may have a drink."

"It may come to that," said Bagheera. Then he sniffed the air and jumped up. "What have you done?" he asked Shere Khan. "That is man smell."

"Yes, it is man," Shere Khan said in a cold voice. "I have just killed one of them."

"What a time to kill a man!" cried Bagheera. "Now they will come and hunt the animals of the Jungle. Was there no other game?"

"I killed for fun and not for food," Shere Khan said. "And now I come to drink. Is anyone going to stop me?"

Hathi had been watching Shere Khan. The elephant was very angry. "You killed for fun?" he asked.

"Yes," Shere Khan answered. "It is my right. You know about my right, Hathi."

"Yes," said the elephant. "I know. Have you finished drinking?"

"For now, yes," Shere Khan said.

"Then go! Only you would kill man this year. The sun presses upon man, too. He has no food

to eat. And he has no water to drink. We are all hurting these days. Man and the Jungle People together. Go!"

Hathi blew the last word through his trunk. It came out so loud it hurt Shere Khan's ears. Shere Khan left in a hurry. What Hathi says, the Jungle People do.

Like the others, Mowgli was afraid of Hathi. Hathi was so much bigger than all of them. But there was something Mowgli wanted to know. "Oh Hathi," he said. "What was Shere Khan talking about? Why is this his right? We must never kill man. The Law says so."

"It is an old, old story," said Hathi. He turned his great head from side to side. "Be quiet along the river and I will tell you."

All was quiet as Hathi began his story. "Listen, my children," he said to all the animals. "You fear many things. And of all things you fear, you are most afraid of man. But once there was no fear in the Jungle. The Jungle People walked together and were afraid of nothing.

"The rains always came in those days. So, there was always enough to eat and drink. The Jungle People ate nothing but leaves and grass and fruit. In those days, there were no houses. There were no farms. The Jungle People knew nothing of man.

"The Head of the Jungle then was Tha, the elephant. Tha had to look after everything in the Jungle. He was so busy that he could not do everything by himself. So, he called on the First of the Tigers to help him.

"The First of the Tigers was as big as I am. He was yellow all over. He had no stripes then. The Jungle People were not afraid of him. He ate only fruit and leaves and grass like the rest of them.

"One day, two deer started fighting over some food. The First of the Tigers tried to stop the fight. But one of the deer hit him with his horns. This made First of the Tigers angry. He lost his head. He jumped upon the deer and killed it.

"Until that day, the Jungle did not know death. That was the first time anything had been killed in the Jungle. 'What have I done?' cried the tiger. He felt so bad that he ran away and hid himself.

"When Tha saw what had happened, he grew very angry. 'Who did this?' he asked the Jungle People. 'Who brought death to the Jungle?'

"But no one knew. Then Tha turned to the Jungle trees. 'You trees were here,' Tha said. 'You know who brought death to the Jungle. When the one who killed the deer walks by, hit him with your branches. Let your blows make black stripes on his skin. He will carry those stripes as long as he lives. And his children will carry them. Then all people will know who brought death to the Jungle.'

"Tha turned back to the Jungle People. 'Part of this was your doing,' he said. 'You must have been fighting with each other or this would never have happened. Now, you will know Fear. From now on you will do what Fear tells you to do.' The Jungle People asked, 'What is Fear?'

" 'You will find out,' Tha said.

"So the Jungle People looked for Fear. They went up and down the Jungle looking for Fear. At last, they found him.

"Fear was sitting in the mouth of a cave. When he saw the Jungle People he stood up. He walked on his back legs. All at once, he called out. His voice made the Jungle People afraid then, just as it does today.

"They tried to run away from Fear. But they were so afraid, they did not even look where they were going. They bumped into each other. Some of them fell and were run over by others. Many of them were hurt.

"After that day, each of the Jungle People stayed with his own kind. Fear had made them afraid of each other. Deer would walk only with other deer. Pigs would eat only with pigs.

"Word of Fear went through the Jungle. Even the First of the Tigers in his hiding place heard about Fear. He said to himself, 'I will break Fear's neck.'

"All that night the tiger hunted for Fear's cave. But as he walked through the Jungle, the trees remembered Tha's words. Every tree the tiger walked under hit him with its branches. Each blow left a black stripe on the tiger's skin. *And those stripes his children wear to this day!*

"At last, the tiger came to the cave. There in its mouth sat Fear. Fear laughed at the tiger's stripes. Fear called the tiger 'The Striped Cat.'

"The First of the Tigers was afraid. He ran howling back to his hiding place. He made so much noise howling that Tha heard him. He followed the sound of the tiger's howls and found his hiding place.

" 'What makes you howl?' asked Tha.

"The tiger looked up at the sky. 'I ran away from Fear,' he said. 'Fear laughed at me. He called me a striped cat. I am *not* striped. This is just mud from the branches of the Jungle trees on my skin.'

"Tha looked at the tiger. One look told him what had happened and why. But all Tha said was, 'If it is only mud, it will wash off. Go wash it off in the river.'

"The tiger did as Tha said. He went to the river and washed. Then he rolled in the grass. But the stripes on his skin would not come off.

"Tha, watching him, laughed.

" 'What have you done to me?' cried the tiger.

" 'You killed the deer,' said Tha. 'You were the first to bring death to the Jungle. So you must wear stripes as long as you live. And your children will wear them after you. With death came fear. Now, the Jungle People are afraid of each other. And they are afraid of you. And you are afraid of Fear.'

"Then the tiger said, 'Remember, once I helped you run the Jungle. Then I did not know Fear. Please, do not let my children know Fear.'

" 'This much I will do for you,' said Tha. 'First I will tell you the name of Fear who sits in a cave. His name is *Man*. Then I shall make one night of each year belong to you. On your night, you and your children will not be afraid of Man. On your night, Man shall be afraid of you. And one more thing. You know what it is to be afraid. So, be kind to Man when he is afraid.'

"The tiger said, 'I will be kind to him.'

"But as the year went by, the tiger grew angry. He remembered the name Man had called him—

30

the Striped Cat. Every time he went to the water hole for a drink he got angry. He could see himself in the water. He saw the black stripes on his skin. The tiger waited for his night.

"When the tiger's night came, he went to find Man. When he found him, everything happened as Tha had said it would. The Man saw the tiger and was afraid. He tried to run away. But he was shaking so hard he could not run. The tiger jumped on him and killed him.

"Just then, Tha came along. He saw what the tiger had done. 'Was that being kind?' asked Tha.

"The tiger laughed. 'I don't care,' he said. 'Look what I have done. I have killed Fear!'

"Tha laughed at him. 'You have killed only one of many. And now Man knows death. He will hunt you until he kills *you*. Your skin will keep his cubs warm. And now, tiger, go home. Your night is over for the year. The sun is coming up now.'

"So that is the story of the tiger's right. To this day, one night each year man fears the tiger. And when the tiger finds man on that night, he kills him.

"Because of the First of the Tigers, man knows death. So, man hunts all the Jungle People. So it is that Fear came to the Jungle."

Hathi had finished his story.

4 MOWGLI LEAVES THE JUNGLE

Mowgli had been with the Wolf Pack more than ten years. Father Wolf had taught him how to live in the Jungle. Baloo had taught him the Law of the Jungle. Bagheera had taught him how to climb trees and how to hunt.

Mowgli could swing on the branches of trees like a monkey. When he was tired, he sat in the sun. When he was hot, he splashed in the Jungle ponds. He grew bigger and he grew strong.

When the wolves met, he took his place at the Council Rock. There he found out something strange. If he looked hard at a wolf, the wolf looked away. He tried it many times. He thought it was fun to make the wolves look away first.

Akela, Head of the Pack, was growing old and weak. Shere Khan knew this, so he made friends with the young wolves. He would give them meat from his kills. Then he would ask them why they followed an old wolf and a man-cub. "I am told that you can not look the man-cub in the eyes," he said. "Are you not as strong as he is?"

Bagheera knew what Shere Khan was up to. "Little Brother," he said to Mowgli, "Shere Khan wants to kill you."

32

"Shere Khan is all loud talk," said Mowgli.

"Akela is old, Little Brother," Bagheera went on. "One day, another wolf will take his place as Head of the Pack. The young wolves feel a man-cub has no place in the Pack. And soon you will be a man."

"Why should a man not run with his brothers?" Mowgli asked. "I follow the Law of the Jungle. There is no wolf in the Pack I have not helped. They know they are my brothers."

"No," Bagheera said, "men are your brothers, not wolves. You must go back to men. Go back before you are killed by the Pack at the Council Rock."

"Why should the wolves wish to kill me?" asked Mowgli.

"Look at me!" said Bagheera. Mowgli looked him in the eyes. Bagheera had to turn his head away.

"*That* is why," he said. "It is because you are better than they are. It is because you are *man*. Not even I can look you in the eyes. And I love you. The others have no love for you. Until now, Akela has kept them from killing you. When he is gone, they will kill you!"

"I did not know these things," said Mowgli.

Then Bagheera had a plan. He jumped up and said, "I have it! Go down to the houses of men in the valley. Take some of the fire that you will see in their houses. Bring it back here. Take it to Council Rock with you. Then the animals will not hurt you, for they are afraid of fire.

So, Mowgli set out for the valley where men had their houses. On his way through the Jungle, he saw the Pack hunting. He stopped running to watch. The Pack was after a deer. Then he heard the young wolves howling. "Akela! Let Akela make the kill," they cried.

As Mowgli watched, Akela jumped at the deer —and missed! No more can Akela be Head of the Pack, Mowgli thought. It is Jungle Law. Once the Head misses his kill, he is finished. And Bagheera said Akela had kept the wolves from killing me. Now they will kill me at the next meeting at Council Rock!

Mowgli did not wait to see more. He ran on to the valley. Once out of the Jungle, he hid himself near a little farm house. No one saw him. After a while, he looked inside the house.

The house had a fire. A boy was feeding the fire with sticks. Mowgli watched the boy pick up a large pan. He filled the pan with coals from the fire and took it outside.

"Is that all fire is?" said Mowgli. "If that cub is not afraid, there must be nothing to fear."

Mowgli ran around the corner of the house and met the boy. He took the pan from the boy's hand. Then he ran back into the Jungle before the boy could stop him.

All that day, Mowgli sat in his cave. He was learning about fire. He would put dry branches on the coals as the boy had done. Then he would blow on them until they caught fire.

That night, a young wolf came to the cave. "They want you at the Council Rock," he said.

Mowgli laughed. He went to the Council Rock still laughing.

Akela lay by the side of his rock. That was to show that he was not Head of the Pack any more. Shere Khan and his young wolf friends were there. Bagheera came and sat close to Mowgli. Mowgli had the fire pan beside him.

When Shere Khan saw Mowgli, he jumped up. "Wolves," he roared, "the man-cub was my meat from the first. Give him to me! If not, you will have no more meat from my hunt."

Old Akela looked at him. "The man-cub has helped us," he said. "Don't hurt him."

"Be quiet, old wolf," roared Shere Khan. "Soon it will be your turn." Then Shere Khan turned to the Pack. "No man-cub should run with the Pack," he said. "Why, not one of you can even look him in the eyes."

"He is a man—a man—a man!" howled the Pack. Most of the wolves walked over to Shere Khan's side.

Bagheera pulled his legs under him, ready to fight. "Now, Little Brother!" he cried to Mowgli.

Mowgli jumped to his feet, the fire pan in his hands. "I have been a wolf with you," he said. "But no more. I do not call you brothers now. I call you dogs. I, man, have brought fire."

He threw the fire pan to the ground. Then he put a dry branch into the hot coals. It caught on fire. The wolves backed off. He waved the branch above his head. The wolves backed away even more. They were very much afraid of fire.

"Good!" said Mowgli. "Now watch. This is how we men take care of dogs."

Mowgli ran up to Shere Khan. The tiger was so afraid he was shaking all over. Mowgli hit him over the head with the branch. Shere Khan

howled and ran off. "Next time I see you," Mowgli called after him, "I will kill you. And I will bring your skin to the Council Rock." He turned back to the wolves. "Now listen to me. Do not kill Akela. That is not my will. Now go."

Mowgli hit right and left with his branch. The wolves howled with fear. They ran into the Jungle after Shere Khan.

"Now, my great friend," said Mowgli, putting his arm around Bagheera. "I will go to live with men. But first, I must say good-by to my mother and father."

He ran to the cave of Mother and Father Wolf. They had been waiting for him. Mowgli sat beside Mother Wolf and began to cry. He did not want to go to live with men. "You will not stop loving me?" he asked.

"Never," said Mother Wolf. "I will always love you. Come to where the Jungle ends when you live with men. We will come there and talk with you. Come soon."

"I will come," said Mowgli. "And some day I will come back to the Council Rock. I will bring the skin of Shere Khan. I will lay it out for all to see. Tell the Jungle People that I will be back."

The sun was coming up when Mowgli left. He walked toward the valley. He was going to live with the strange things called men.

5 TIGER! TIGER!

So, Mowgli left the Jungle to live with men. At one end of the valley stood a little town. There were about 40 small houses in the town. Around the town was a big fence.

"So," Mowgli said, looking at the fence, "men are afraid of the Jungle People."

A farmer on his way to his fields saw Mowgli. He gave a shout and ran back toward the town. In a few minutes, he came back, bringing people with him. When they saw Mowgli, they all cried out in fear.

Then a fat man pushed his way through the shouting people. He was the head of the town. He walked up to Mowgli and looked him over. "Is this what you are afraid of?" he asked. "This is nothing but a wolf-child. Look how long his hair is. And he wears no clothes. He must have run away from the Jungle."

One man cried out, "Messua! He looks like your son who was carried off by a tiger!"

A pretty woman with gold rings in her ears pushed her way toward Mowgli. "Let me see! Let me see!" she cried. "Oh, how thin he is! But he does look like my boy. Yes. It is my son!"

The fat man faced the people. "After all these years," he said, "Messua's son has come back to us. Don't be afraid of him. Come. Let's get back to work."

The pretty woman pulled Mowgli by the arm. She took him into her house. There was a nice fire in the kitchen. Its light made her gold rings shine. She gave Mowgli some milk and bread. Then she tried to talk to him.

Mowgli did not know what she was saying. I must learn man's talk, he thought. So, when Messua talked to him, he said each word after her. By dark, he had learned the names of many things in the house.

That night, Mowgli could not sleep inside the house. He did not like having a roof over his head. Poor thing, thought Messua, he has never had a bed. I'll let him sleep where he wants. If he *is* my son, he will not run away.

So, Mowgli went out to the fields. He found some soft grass and lay down. Just as he was falling asleep, he heard a noise. A soft, wet nose pressed into his face.

It was Gray Brother, one of Mother Wolf's cubs. "Wake up, Little Brother," said the cub. "I bring word from the Jungle."

Mowgli sat up and threw his arms around Gray Brother's neck. "What has happened?" he asked.

"Your fire branch hurt Shere Khan," Gray Brother said. "He has run away and no one knows where he is. But before he went, he told the Pack he would be back. He said he would come back and kill you."

Mowgli ground his teeth together. "We will see who gets killed," he said. "Thank you, Gray Brother, for coming to tell me."

The wolf sat beside Mowgli for a minute. "Are we not still brothers, Mowgli?" he asked.

Mowgli rubbed Gray Brother's ears. "Yes," he told him. "I love you and all in our cave. But I am finished with the Pack."

"You may find men no better than the Wolf Pack," Gray Brother said. "But what will you do about Shere Khan?"

"Do not fear. I will not walk into Shere Khan's mouth," said Mowgli. He pointed toward the Jungle. A small hill could be seen. "See that hill, Gray Brother? If Shere Khan comes back, I want you to sit on it. I'll watch every day. When I see you on the hill, I'll meet you there."

Many weeks went by. Mowgli was busy trying to learn the ways of men. But it was hard. His skin did not like the clothes that Messua made him wear. And he thought farming was hard work. "Hunting is better," he said to himself.

Buldeo was the man who did the farmers' hunting. Mowgli did not get along with him. Buldeo thought he knew all about the Jungle.

But Mowgli thought Buldeo knew nothing at all about the Jungle People.

One night the farmers were talking together. Buldeo began to talk about Shere Khan. "He looks like a tiger," Buldeo said. "But he is not a tiger. He is a ghost who kills men. He is the ghost of a bad man who once lived here."

"That is child's talk," Mowgli said. "I know that tiger. Shere Khan is no ghost. Yes, he kills men. But he kills cows, too. Is he also the ghost of a cow?"

Buldeo was so angry his face grew red. His voice was hard when he talked to Mowgli. "Boy," he said, "you know so much. Why don't you go hunt the tiger?"

All the men laughed at the thought of a boy hunting a tiger.

"That tiger's head will bring you a hundred pieces of gold," Buldeo said. "But you will never get the gold. The tiger is a ghost. Now be quiet before your betters, know-nothing."

The farmers did not like Mowgli any better than Buldeo did. And Mowgli did not like them. One day the head of the town said, "You, Jungle Boy. From now on, take care of the water buffaloes."

So, Mowgli began to take care of the water

buffaloes. He loved the work. Early each morning, he would go out with the water buffaloes. Riding Rama, the head buffalo, he took them to the river near the Jungle. There the grass grew long and sweet. On the way, he always looked for Gray Brother on the hill. At night, he took the water buffaloes back to the farms.

The day came when Mowgli saw Gray Brother sitting on the hill. That was the sign that Shere Khan had come back. Mowgli headed Rama toward the hill. When they were close, Mowgli jumped off Rama's back. He ran up to Gray Brother.

"Shere Khan came last night," said Gray Brother.

"Has he had anything to eat?" Mowgli asked.

"A fat pig," Gray Brother told him. "He killed it this morning. He has had water, too."

"That is bad for him," laughed Mowgli. "He should not eat and drink before he hunts! Now he will be sleepy and slow. Does he think I will wait for him to sleep it off?"

Then Mowgli pointed to the water buffaloes. "I need their help. But I don't know their talk. So, we will have to drive them. Do you think we can do it?"

Gray Brother said, "We will have help."

Just then, Akela jumped out from behind a rock.

Mowgli clapped his hands. "Akela!" he cried. "How glad I am to see you. We need your help. Here is what we will do. You and I, Akela, will take some of the buffaloes with us. We will go up the river until we get behind Shere Khan. Then we will make our buffaloes run toward him.

"Gray Brother, you take the rest of the buffaloes down the river. Wait until you see us coming. Then, get your buffaloes moving. Make a lot of noise. I want them to run straight toward us as fast as they can. Shere Khan will be caught between your buffaloes and ours. He will be tired. He can not swim the river. We will have him."

Gray Brother and Akela ran up to the water buffaloes. Even the smell of a wolf makes buffaloes afraid. And here were two wolves, howling and showing their teeth. In no time at all, the buffaloes did just what Mowgli wanted.

If Mowgli was to get behind Shere Khan, he must not wake him up. The buffaloes must not make a lot of noise. So, Mowgli told Akela to drop far behind. When the buffaloes could not smell the wolf any more, they slowed down. Mowgli quieted them with his voice.

At last, Mowgli spotted Shere Khan's hiding

place. It was in a ring of tall elephant grass. He could see Shere Khan, fast asleep.

Mowgli cupped his hands around his mouth. "Shere Khan!" he shouted.

"Who calls?" asked the tiger in a sleepy voice.

"I, Mowgli the Frog. Akela and I are on a tiger hunt. Wake up, Shere Khan!"

Mowgli pointed Rama toward Shere Khan's hiding place. "Akela!" he cried. "Get these buffaloes moving."

Akela gave the hunting call of a hungry wolf. The buffaloes were afraid. Rama began to run. The other buffaloes followed. As the buffaloes closed in, they smelled Shere Khan. The tiger smell made them go wild. They mooed with fear. They seemed to fly over the ground. There was no stopping them.

Shere Khan was on his feet. He saw a sea of horns coming at him. There was only one way for him to go—down the river.

Shere Khan ran as he had never run before. Then he saw Gray Brother's buffaloes. They were running straight for him. Behind them, Gray Brother was running and howling.

Shere Khan looked from side to side. Buffaloes were running at him from both sides. There was no way out. He gave a roar of fear. The buffaloes, horns down, closed in.

And that was the end of Shere Khan.

The buffaloes were still wild with fear. They were bumping into each other. "Quick, Akela!" Mowgli called. "Break them up. They will start fighting each other."

"There, there, my children," Mowgli called to the buffaloes. "It is all over."

At last, they got the buffaloes away from what was left of Shere Khan. Mowgli began to skin the tiger. He was almost finished when Buldeo came running up.

"What is this?" Buldeo asked. "The tiger! No, it can not be. The tiger! Well, well. There are a hundred gold pieces on his head. You bad boy! You let the buffaloes run off. But it is all right this time. I may even give you a gold piece."

Mowgli laughed. "So, Buldeo, you will take the tiger. And you will take the money. And I should thank you for one gold piece? I think not! I need this skin for my own use."

"I'll teach you to talk like that to me," Buldeo said. "You will not get any gold at all. I'll give you a knock on the head. Now be off."

Mowgli went back to his skinning. "You are all noise, like the Monkey People," he told Buldeo. "Here, Akela! This man talks too much."

All at once, Buldeo found himself face down on the grass. He rolled over and looked up. Akela was standing over him. His teeth were close to Buldeo's nose.

Buldeo lay as still as he could for fear the wolf would kill him. Mowgli must be a sorcerer, he thought. How else could he make wolves do what he says?

"Please let me up," Buldeo cried.

Mowgli smiled.

"I am an old man," cried Buldeo. His voice was shaking with fear. "I did not know you were a sorcerer. May I get up? Or will you tell the wolf to kill me?"

"Next time, stay out of my way," Mowgli told him. "Akela, let him go."

Buldeo jumped up and ran as fast as he could. And he kept running until he was home. There he told the people that Mowgli was a sorcerer. "He can put a spell on things. He talks to wolves. I saw him with my own eyes. The wolves do what he says. He will kill us all."

It was almost dark when Mowgli finished skinning Shere Khan. He hid the skin in an old log. Then he got Gray Brother and Akela to help him drive the buffaloes home.

As they came near the town, Mowgli saw the farmers. They were waiting for him outside the fence. He thought they wanted to thank him for killing the tiger.

Then Mowgli saw that the farmers were throwing things. Stones came flying through the air. One hit Mowgli on the arm.

"Wolf cub! Sorcerer!" the farmers shouted. "Go back to the Jungle."

Messua pulled away from the other people and ran out to Mowgli. "Oh, my son!" she cried. "My son! Buldeo says you are a sorcerer. I don't believe it. But the rest of them do. They are afraid you will put a spell on them. Run away or they will kill you."

"Come back, Messua," the farmers called. "Come back or we will stone you, too."

Another stone hit Mowgli. He gave a short, hard laugh. "The Wolf Pack did not want me because I am a man," he said. "Now these people don't want me because I am a wolf. Don't cry, Messua. I am not a sorcerer." Mowgli put his arms around her. "Thank you for being so good to me. I'll go now. Good-by."

Mowgli turned and walked away. "No more sleeping in houses for me, Akela," he said. "I will go back to the Jungle."

So Mowgli headed for the Jungle with Akela and Gray Brother. On the way, he picked up the tiger's skin. "I am going to take it to the Council Rock," he said. "I will show them that Mowgli's word is good."

"Little Brother!" called a voice as Mowgli came to the Council Rock. It was Bagheera. "I am glad you are back," he said. "The Jungle was not the same without you."

Akela called all the Wolf Pack to the Council Rock. Akela was not the Head of the Pack any more. But the wolves still came when they heard his voice.

"Look well!" cried Mowgli to the wolves. "Have I not kept my word?" Then he sang and danced on the skin of Shere Khan.

"Be the Head of the Pack!" cried the wolves to Mowgli.

But Mowgli gave them all a hard look. "No," he said. "Both the Man Pack and the Wolf Pack threw me out. Now I will hunt alone in the Jungle."

6 LETTING IN THE JUNGLE

When he went back to the Jungle, Mowgli thought he had finished with men. But it was not to be. The very next afternoon, Bagheera and Akela came to Mother Wolf's cave.

"Mowgli," Akela called. "Buldeo is hunting you. He is on your trail! Come and see."

Mowgli and his four wolf brothers followed Bagheera and Akela. They moved through the Jungle without making a sound.

This is more than could be said for Buldeo. Mowgli could hear him even before he saw him. The old man was talking to himself. He was saying how hard it was to trail Mowgli.

Mowgli laughed. Here he and Bagheera and five wolves were right under Buldeo's nose. And the old man did not know it. Men have eyes and don't see, thought Mowgli.

Then Mowgli heard more noises. He saw four farmers coming along the trail. They walked up to Buldeo.

"Hello," said one of the farmers. "We are coming from another town to pay your town a visit."

"Well, you had better be careful," said Buldeo. "There is a sorcerer in this Jungle. I am hunting him now." And Buldeo told the farmers all about Mowgli. He ended the story by saying, "He can turn into a wolf when he wants to. I have seen it with my own eyes.

"The mother of the sorcerer lives in our town. We have her tied up. We are sure she is a sorcerer, too. We will kill her right after I kill the boy."

Buldeo's story made the farmers afraid. But telling the story made Buldeo even more afraid than they were. It was late in the afternoon. The sun would soon be going down.

Buldeo looked into the dark Jungle around him. He did not want to stay there alone in the dark. "I—I think I had better go with you to my town," he said. "Then, if you should meet the sorcerer, I'll—I'll be there to take care of you." Buldeo tried his best not to look afraid.

As the men went along the trail through the Jungle, Mowgli turned to his friends. "We can not let them kill Messua," he said. "I'll run to the Man Pack. You slow down Buldeo. Sing the hunting call to him and the farmers. They will be too afraid to move."

The black panther cried a long, loud "Good hunting!" Gray Brother answered with his own hunting call. Then Akela and the other wolves cried, "Good hunting to us all!"

Buldeo must have thought there were a hundred animals after him. He ran around and around, trying to look every place at once. The farmers were holding on to each other and shaking with fear.

Mowgli laughed. Then he ran as fast as he could for the town. He ran straight to Messua's house and looked in the window. There, tied to a chair, was Messua. Mowgli climbed through the window and hurried to cut the ropes.

When Messua saw Mowgli climbing through her window, she began to cry. "Now I know you are my son," she said. "You have come to save me."

She had been hit with sticks and stones. The blows had cut her face and arms. She was afraid and she was crying.

It took Mowgli a long time to quiet her. "Why did they do this?" he asked.

"Because you are my son," said Messua. "But most of all because I own many buffaloes and much gold. They would like to kill me and take my animals and my gold. That is why they say that I am a sorcerer, too."

Just then, the sound of shouting and talking came from outside. "That must be Buldeo and the farmers," Mowgli said. "Buldeo will have a great story to tell about Jungle ghosts. But when it is over, they will be coming for you. I must get you out of here."

"My son," Messua said, "there is a city 40 miles from here. It is called Khanhiwara. The people there do not believe in ghosts and sorcerers. If I could get to Khanhiwara, I would be all right. But I would have to go through the Jungle to get there. And I am afraid of the wild animals."

Mowgli put his arms around Messua. "It is my Jungle," he said. "The animals are my friends. Go to Khanhiwara. No one will hurt you."

Mowgli helped Messua climb through the window. The night air made her feel better. But she was still hurt and tired. Mowgli took her across the fields to where the Jungle began.

"Don't be afraid," he said, holding her hand. "You may hear the Jungle People calling to each other. But they will only be watching out for you. You had better start now. I have to stay behind and take care of Buldeo."

Messua threw her arms around Mowgli one last time. Then she started along the trail toward Khanhiwara. At a sign from Mowgli, two of his wolf brothers followed her. Messua would have two strong wolves to see her through the Jungle.

Mowgli ran back to Messua's house. Bagheera went with him. They heard Buldeo and the other farmers shouting. "Kill the sorcerer!" they shouted. "Throw her in the fire! Kill her! Kill her! Let's go get her now."

Bagheera looked up at Mowgli. "Let them find me in the woman's house," he said. "I don't think they will throw *me* in the fire."

Bagheera jumped through the window into Messua's house. He lay down on the floor and faced the door. In a few minutes, the farmers were at the door. Bagheera could hear them pushing each other. Each wanted to be the first to get his hands on Messua. Buldeo shouted, "It is my right!" He threw the door open—and saw Bagheera.

For a minute, no one moved. There was not even a sound. Then Buldeo and the other farmers turned, crying out with fear. They ran as fast as they could for their own houses. There was the sound of one door after another banging shut.

Bagheera jumped back through the window and stood by Mowgli. There was not a farmer to be seen. "They will stay in their houses until morning," said Bagheera. "You can be sure of that. The woman will be far away by that time. Now, Little Brother, we are finished. Let's go home and have nothing more to do with the Man Pack."

"We are not finished," said Mowgli. "I want them out of this valley. Where does Hathi, the elephant, feed these days?"

"Who can answer for Hathi?" asked Bagheera.

"Find him," Mowgli said. "Tell him to come here to me."

"Little Brother," Bagheera answered, "one does not say 'come' and 'go' to Hathi. Remember, he is Head of the Jungle."

"Very well," said Mowgli. "But I have a Master Word for Hathi. Tell him to come because of *Bhurtpore*."

"Bhurtpore," said Bagheera. "Bhurtpore. All

right, I'll go. I would give a fat deer to hear the Master Word that could make Hathi come."

Bagheera was not gone long. When he came back, Hathi was walking behind him. "It *was* a Master Word," said Bagheera to Mowgli.

Hathi had brought along his three sons. The four of them had been feeding on the sweet river grass when Bagheera found them.

Hathi threw his trunk above his head. "Good hunting, Mowgli!" he said.

"I heard a story," Mowgli said, "about an elephant who fell into a trap. The trap's teeth cut the elephant from his foot all the way up his leg." Mowgli ran his hand up Hathi's gray leg.

"The next day," Mowgli went on, "men came to take the elephant from the trap. But the elephant was strong and got away. And I remember now, this elephant had three sons. He and his sons went to Bhurtpore. That is where the men who trapped him lived. What happened to Bhurtpore, Hathi?"

"We ran over the farmer's fields," said Hathi. "We knocked down the men's houses. We killed most of the farmers. The others ran away. In a little while, the Jungle moved into the farmers' fields. It began to grow until it covered the fields and the houses. And today no one knows where Bhurtpore once stood."

"Hathi," said Mowgli, "the Man Pack in this valley is bad. They want to throw one of their own kind, a woman, into the fire. Help me get them out of the valley."

"Will there be killing?" asked Hathi. "I do not want to smell blood again."

"No," Mowgli answered. "I don't want them killed. I want to drive them away so they will never come back."

"All right, Mowgli," said Hathi, "I'll help you. It will take us a little time. But we will let the Jungle into the valley."

Hathi went north. Each of his three sons went off another way. For two long days, they walked without stopping. Word started going through the Jungle that there was good feeding in the valley. No one knew who started the story. But all the Jungle People heard it. The deer and the pigs were the first to start toward the valley. Then the Monkey People, the wild buffaloes, the foxes, and all the birds followed. In ten days, the hills around the valley were covered with animals.

Hathi and his three sons came back. They walked down into the valley toward the farmers' fields. Many of the animals followed them right away. And the wolves were driving the others after them.

The Jungle People started feeding in the farmers' fields. Hathi and his sons moved on. They pushed their way through the fence into the town.

The farmers looked out of their windows. They wondered what was making all the noise.

Then they saw the four elephants coming toward them. Behind the elephants, they could see the Jungle People feeding in their fields.

Who can fight the Jungle? The farmers knew that by morning there would be nothing left of their fields. And the elephants were coming straight for them!

Before Hathi and his sons could knock down the houses, the farmers ran. Hathi saw to it that they would never come back. As soon as a family left its house, he would knock it down. Then, there was nothing for the farmers to come back to.

When the houses were almost all knocked down, it started raining. Mowgli stood in the rain patting Hathi's trunk. "The Jungle will make this valley clean again," he said. "We have let it in. Now it will grow over everything."

"All in good time," answered Hathi. "First, this last house must come down. All together, my children," he said to his sons. "With the head! Now, push!"

In a few weeks, the first soft, green grass began to grow. It covered every place where houses and fields had been. Soon after, the Jungle took root. No one would have known that men had ever lived in the valley.

7 THE KING'S ANKUS

It was the time of year when Kaa, the rock snake, got a new skin. His old skin dried up and he came out of it. Mowgli came to wish him well with his new skin.

Kaa was glad to see Mowgli. "How does my new coat look?" he asked.

"It is beautiful," said Mowgli. He patted the fresh, new skin.

Kaa looked pleased. "Still, it needs water," he said. "A new skin never comes to full color until the first washing. Let's go take a bath."

Sliding over the ground, Kaa headed for his Jungle pond. Mowgli ran along beside him. Kaa loved to swim as much as Mowgli. The two of them swam in the water for a long time. Then they climbed out of the pond and rested in the warm sun.

After a while, Kaa opened his eyes. "Mowgli," he said, "the other day I went hunting in the Cold Lairs. I came upon an old white cobra. He showed me some strange things in a hole."

Mowgli turned on his side so he could see Kaa. "Was it something to eat?" he asked.

"No," said Kaa. "It was not something to eat. I don't know what it was. It was cold and hard and hurt my teeth. But the white cobra said men loved it above all else."

"Let me have a look at it," said Mowgli. "I lived with the Man Pack for a while. I might know what it is."

Mowgli and Kaa set off for the Cold Lairs. Night fell before they saw the first building of the lost city. With Kaa beside him, Mowgli was not afraid of the Monkey People. But the Monkey People were not there that night.

Kaa took Mowgli down steps that went deep under the ground. It was cold and dark when they came to the last step.

"We are in a large room," said Mowgli to Kaa. "But I can not see anything."

"How about me?" asked a voice in the dark. Then Mowgli saw a big cobra in front of him. It was bigger than any Mowgli had ever seen. It was almost 8 feet long. And it was as white as milk.

"We be of one blood, you and I," Mowgli said at once.

The cobra's head rocked from side to side on its long neck. "Tell me of the great city," he said, "the city of a hundred elephants. Tell me of the city of gold. I can not hear well any more.

I don't remember when I last heard noises from the city above me."

"I told you about that," Kaa said. "There are no more people in the city."

"Then who is he?" asked the white cobra, pointing his head at Mowgli. "He stands before me and is not afraid. He talks our talk through the mouth of a man."

Mowgli answered for himself. "I am of the Jungle," he said. "The wolves are my people and Kaa is my brother. My name is Mowgli. Father of cobras, who are you?"

"I watch over the King's treasure. I bring death to those who try to take it away from here. Many years back, the King sent his men down here to dig this room. After many days, they finished digging. Then, they carried his treasure down here. I was brought here to watch over it.

"In all the world, there can be no treasure like this. From time to time, men have tried to take away the treasure. I have killed them all. Now you two come here with lies. You tell me that the city is no more. Still, I will do this much for you. I'll show you something you have never seen before. Look over there!"

Mowgli followed the white cobra's eyes. He saw something shining on the floor. He went to look at it. "Oh," he said. "It is only gold. The Man Pack that lived in the valley had some of it."

The floor was covered with gold pieces. Around the walls were many bags filled with gold. Other bags were filled with bright-colored stones. There were red, green, blue, yellow, and white stones. Mowgli had seen two or three such stones in the town. But those he had seen were small. These were large. And there were hundreds and hundreds of them in the bags.

Mowgli knew that the Man Pack loved these stones even more than gold. But to Mowgli, a stone was a stone. And he had never seen any use for gold. But at last something caught his eye. It was an ankus about three feet long.

An ankus is a stick that men use to drive elephants. Like a knife, it has a point on one end. And just below the point, it also has a hook. So, an ankus can hurt an elephant in two ways. This ankus had been made for the King. It was covered with gold and colored stones. Down both sides were pictures of men catching elephants.

The white cobra had been watching Mowgli's face. "It is beautiful, don't you think?" he asked.

"Yes," Mowgli answered. "I would like to see its pictures in the sun. Give me the ankus, and I'll bring you frogs to eat."

The white cobra's red eyes began to shine in the dark. "Oh, I'll give it to you," he said. "You may have everything in this room—until you try to leave."

"But," said Mowgli, "I want to go now. This place is cold and dark."

"Those who come for the treasure never leave this room," said the cobra.

"I don't want your treasure," Mowgli answered. "I don't fight the Snake People. And I gave you the Master Words."

"There are no Master Words here," said the white cobra.

Kaa pushed his head between Mowgli and the cobra. "Who asked me to bring him here," Kaa asked.

"I did," the old cobra answered. "I had not seen a man in a long time."

"Then let's have no talk of killing," said Kaa.

"Listen, you long, fat snake," said the cobra. "Keep out of this. If I bit your neck, that would put an end to you. No man comes here and leaves again. His bones stay with me to watch over the King's treasure."

"You white worm!" Kaa cried out. "I tell you that the King and the city are no more."

"That may be," said the cobra. "But there is still the treasure. Wait a while, Kaa of the Rocks. Watch me make the boy run."

Mowgli put his hand on Kaa's head. "The white thing knows only men of the Man Pack," he said in Kaa's ear. "He does not know me. He has asked for this. I will let him have it!"

Mowgli had been standing with the ankus. With a quick move, he threw the ankus to the ground. It caught the cobra's neck between its point and its hook.

"Kill him!" cried Kaa.

"No," said Mowgli. "I kill only for food."
Mowgli held the cobra behind its neck. He
pushed open its mouth with his knife. "Look!"
he cried. There were no poison bags inside the
cobra's mouth. The cobra was so old that all of
his poison had dried up.

"Is this how you watch over the King's
treasure?" laughed Mowgli.

"I am too old to live," said the cobra. "Kill
me."

"There has been too much talk of killing,"
said Mowgli. "We will go now. But because I
could have killed you, I'll take the gold ankus."

"It will kill you," the cobra said. "It brings death! You will not keep it long, Jungle Man. And he who takes it from you also will not keep it long. I am not strong any more. But the ankus will do my work."

Mowgli and Kaa left the room and went up the steps. The fresh air felt good on their faces. They were glad to be out in the Jungle again.

It was morning when they got to their own part of the Jungle. "I am hungry," said Kaa. "Will you hunt with me?"

"No," said Mowgli. He moved the ankus so that the morning light caught on the bright stones. "Look! It shines like Bagheera's eyes. It is beautiful. I must show it to him. Good hunting!"

Mowgli skipped off, swinging the ankus. He found Bagheera at the river. Mowgli showed him the ankus and told him its story. Then, he asked, "Bagheera, what do men use this thing for?"

"Men use it to hit elephants," said Bagheera. "A blow from the ankus can make blood run from an elephant's skin. I have seen it happen. That ankus must have felt the blood of many elephants."

"I don't want it then," cried Mowgli. He threw the shining ankus at the foot of a big tree. Then he rubbed his hands on the grass to clean them. "Now my hands are clean of death," he said.

"They are clean, Little Brother," said Bagheera. "And now it is time to sleep. Come. My place is not far from here."

When Mowgli woke up, he remembered the ankus. "I'll look at the beautiful ankus just once more," he said. But when he went to the tree, the ankus was gone.

"Bagheera!" Mowgli called. "The ankus is gone."

Bagheera came to look. "A man took it," said Bagheera. "Here is his trail."

"Good!" said Mowgli. "Now we will see if the white cobra was right. If the ankus brings death, the man will be killed. Let's follow his trail and see."

Mowgli and Bagheera followed the man's trail all morning. It took them many miles through the Jungle. At last, they found the man. But death had found him first. He lay on the ground with an arrow in his back. And the ankus was gone.

"The cobra was old, Little Brother," said Bagheera. "But he was right. And look! Here is a new trail going north. Another man took the ankus."

"He must be afraid," Mowgli said. "The trail shows that he is running."

This trail was not a long one. They found the man not far away. Like the first man, he had been killed. His head had been pushed in with a rock.

"The Father of Cobras knows men well," said Mowgli, shaking his head. "I should not have made fun of him. Bagheera, look here! Now we have a trail of four men wearing shoes."

For a long time they trailed the four men. Then Bagheera saw a red coat on the ground and went over to look. "The ankus has been at work again," he said. "This one has also been killed."

"That makes three men the ankus has killed," Mowgli said.

"Let's see what else happens," said Bagheera. And they took up the trail again.

They had not gone far when they heard Chil, the kite. He was singing the Death Song. Then they saw three men on the ground under a tree.

"There is no blood on them," Bagheera said. "What killed them?"

"Look!" said Mowgli. They have bread in their hands. They must have been killed while they were eating."

Mowgli took a piece of the bread and smelled it. Making a face, he cried out, "Poison! Before these men killed the last man, he gave them poisoned bread."

"Don't men smell poison under their noses?" asked Bagheera.

"They have noses and don't smell. Just as they have eyes and don't see," Mowgli answered.

Bagheera looked up at Mowgli. "What now?" he asked. "Will you and I kill each other for the ankus?"

"I don't think it works on us," Mowgli said. He picked up the ankus. "We don't care about the bright stones. Still, I'll take it back to the Father of Cobras. I don't love the Man Pack. But I don't want six of them killing each other every night."

The white cobra was sitting in his room under the Cold Lairs. He felt bad about his lost ankus. Just then, something flew through the dark and dropped beside him with a ringing noise. It was the ankus!

"Father of Cobras," called Mowgli. "Find a young cobra to help you watch over the King's treasure."

"Oh, it is back again!" cried the white cobra. "But why do you still live?"

"I don't know," Mowgli answered. "But that thing has killed six times in one night. Let the King's ankus out no more."

8 THE RED DOGS

Not even the Jungle People can stop the slow marching of time. Time killed Father and Mother Wolf. Mowgli cried the Death Song over them.

Baloo grew old. Even Bagheera was not as fast on his kill any more. Time turned Akela's coat from gray to milk white. Mowgli had to hunt for him.

Phao, a friend of Akela's, became Head of the Pack. Mowgli did not run with the Pack. But sometimes he would go to the Council Rock.

One night across the Jungle came a wild cry. It had the sound of death in it. It hit Mowgli and his four wolf brothers like a blow. The wolves showed their teeth. Mowgli's hand went for his knife. Then Mowgli and the wolves ran to the Council Rock.

Phao and all the other wolves were there before them. They asked each other what had made the Death Cry. Then they heard tired feet running on the rocks. A wolf came running up. But he was not one of the wolves of the Pack. He had been hurt. He could not use one of his paws. There was blood on his side.

"The dogs! The Red Dogs!" cried the new wolf. Then he fell at Mowgli's feet.

"What happened?" Phao asked the new wolf.

"I am Won-tolla," said the wolf. "I do not belong to any Pack. The Red Dogs came to my hunting ground from the east. They must have killed all the game there. While I was out hunting, they killed my mate and three cubs. I went after them and found them."

"How many?" asked Mowgli.

"I don't know," answered Won-tolla. "Three of them will kill no more. But there were too many of them for me. I had to run from them as if I were a pig."

The Pack knew that even the tiger feared the red hunting dogs of the east. These dogs drive straight through the Jungle. What animals they meet, they kill. They are not as big as wolves. But they are very strong. And they run hundreds to a Pack. Even Hathi is afraid of them.

Akela came over to Mowgli. "We will go after the Red Dogs. It will be good hunting—and my last," he said. "But you have many more days and nights to live. Go north, Little Brother. If any of us live through the fight with the Red Dogs, he shall bring you word."

Mowgli rubbed Akela's head. "My father and mother were wolves," he said. "And there is one old white wolf who is both father and mother to me." He looked around him. "When the Red Dogs come, Mowgli and the Wolf Pack will hunt them together. Let the Wolf Pack get ready. I go to see how many Red Dogs there are."

Mowgli hurried off. He was busy thinking as he ran. He was not looking where he was going. And so, he fell over Kaa, who lay waiting for deer.

"What are you doing?" asked Kaa in an angry voice. "Now every deer for a mile around knows where Kaa is."

Mowgli picked himself up. "Don't be angry, Kaa," he said. "I came looking for you. There is no one in the Jungle who knows so much."

"Well, what do you want?" asked Kaa. He sounded pleased.

Petting the snake's long neck, Mowgli told him what had happened. At the end of the story he said, "I need a plan for hunting the Red Dogs. That is why I came to you."

"Then be quiet and let me think," said Kaa. He lay still and thought of everything he had ever seen. He thought back to the day he came out of his egg. At last he said, "I will show you how to hunt the Red Dogs."

Kaa took Mowgli along the river to a deep gorge. From the high rocks on the sides of the gorge came a bad smell. The river ran fast and wild through the gorge.

"This is the Place of Death," said Mowgli, sniffing. "Why did you bring me here?"

"We are all right," Kaa said. "The Little People are asleep. They will not wake up until morning."

The Little People are the wild black bees of India. They made their homes in the rocks of the gorge. There the bees made their honey. There they laid their eggs and gave food to their young. All who came near were killed by hundreds and hundreds of angry little bees. That is why the Little People are called the Masters of the Jungle.

"Once when I was little," said Kaa, "I saw a

strange thing. A deer came running from the east with a Wolf Pack on its trail. Not knowing our Jungle, the deer ran this way. He came to the top of the gorge and jumped into the river.

"The Little People were made very angry by the noise. Hundreds of them flew at the Pack. Some of the Pack jumped into the river after the deer. Before they hit the water, the Little People had killed them. Those who stayed on the rocks above were also killed by the Little People. But they did not kill the deer."

"Why?" asked Mowgli.

"Because he came first," Kaa answered. "He jumped into the water before the Little People knew what was happening."

"The deer lived?" Mowgli asked.

"Well," said Kaa, "the Little People did not kill him. But the river did. The water here is too strong for most. It carried him under.

"But he did not have an old, fat, yellow snake waiting in the river to save him. A snake could wait in the river and save a man from the water. Yes. Kaa would wait though all the Red Dogs of India were on his trail."

Mowgli patted Kaa's head. "Kaa knows more than all the Jungle People," he said.

"So many have said," Kaa answered. "But look, can you make the Red Dogs follow you?"

"Oh, they will follow," said Mowgli. "I will say things to them to make them angry."

"Good!" said Kaa. "Even the Little People can not kill all the Red Dogs. There are too many of them. But the river will kill more. And those it does not kill will be carried down the river. The Wolf Pack can wait and finish them off. Now, go and look over the ground where you will be running. Remember, if you fall, the Red Dogs will kill you. I'll go and tell the Wolf Pack what to do."

Next day, late in the afternoon, Mowgli went looking for the Red Dogs. He could hear them calling their Death Cry. As soon as he saw them, he climbed a tree. There were more than two hundred Red Dogs. They were coming toward him. Noses to the ground, they were following Won-tolla's trail.

"Who said you could hunt here?" shouted Mowgli from his tree.

The Head of the Pack looked up. "This Jungle is now ours," he said.

"Dogs! Red Dogs!" Mowgli laughed. "Go home and eat frogs!"

The Red Dogs were growing angry. Soon they would be so angry they would want to kill him. That was just as Mowgli planned. He sat down on a tree branch. Then he told the Red Dogs what he thought of them. His words made them very angry. They began jumping up, trying to catch hold of Mowgli. The Head of the Pack jumped close to Mowgli's branch. Mowgli caught him by the neck with his right hand. With his left hand, he used his knife to cut off the dog's tail. Then he let the dog fall to the ground.

That was all Mowgli needed to do. Now the Pack would stay by his tree until the end. They would stay until he killed them or they killed him.

The sun was going down. Soon the Little People would be going to sleep. Mowgli jumped like a monkey to the next tree. Then he jumped to another. The dogs followed as Mowgli went from tree to tree.

Soon Mowgli came to the end of the trees. From there to the gorge was open ground. He jumped down and ran like the wind for the Bee Rocks.

Giving their Death Cry, the Red Dogs went after him. They were sure the boy was theirs at last.

The Little People had gone to sleep for the night. But the noise Mowgli and the dogs made woke them. Their buzzing grew strong. Mowgli ran as he had never run before.

He came to the top of the gorge. Without stopping for a minute, he jumped feet first down into the river. The water caught him and almost carried him away. But Kaa was there to save him. Mowgli held on to Kaa as the river began to pull him down. Kaa's strong tail held them both to a rock.

Mowgli and Kaa saw the Red Dogs jumping into the river. But before landing in the water, each dog was covered with angry bees. The buzzing became an angry roar.

"We had better not stay here," said Kaa. He began swimming with Mowgli down the river.

After he had gone about a mile, Kaa stopped. They could not hear the angry buzzing any more. "The Little People have gone back to sleep," he said. "The Wolf Pack is just down the river, Mowgli. I am going to leave you here. See. The river is carrying the dogs that still live down to you. Good hunting, Little Brother."

With that, Kaa went swimming off.

The bees and the river had killed many of the Red Dogs. But there were still many of them left. Those who lived swam down the river with the Head of the Pack. They spotted a place where they could climb out of the river. But as soon as they climbed out, the wolves were on them.

It was hard hunting. There were many more dogs than wolves. But the howling wolves flew at the dogs. Mowgli was there to help. His knife never stopped its work.

The Head of the Red Dogs came running up. Won-tolla jumped for his neck. Won-tolla had lost much blood and was very weak. But his teeth closed shut on the dog's neck. The Head of the Red Dogs fell over and lay still. Then Won-tolla fell on top of him.

"You have won your Blood Right!" Mowgli cried. "Sing the song, Won-tolla."

"He hunts no more," said Gray Brother. "Old Akela, too, has ended his hunting days."

"The Red Dogs go!" shouted Phao. "After them! Kill them!"

The dogs ran into the river and into the Jungle. They ran any place to get away from the wolves.

"The Blood Right! The Blood Right!" shouted Mowgli. "They have killed Akela. Don't let any of them get away."

After the fighting was finished, Mowgli found Akela. Death had not quite come to the old wolf. But he was wet with his own blood.

"I told you this would be my last hunt," said Akela in a weak voice. "Little Brother, help me to my feet. I want to meet death like one who is Head of the Wolf Pack."

Being careful not to hurt him, Mowgli helped Akela to stand. With his head held high, Akela sang his own Death Song. The song went ringing through the Jungle. At the last "Good Hunting!," Akela jumped high into the air. Death took him before he fell to the ground.

"Good hunting, oh best of wolves!" said Mowgli.

The Red Dogs had killed Akela and many other wolves. And the Red Dogs' teeth had hurt each of the wolves. But the wolves had won their Blood Right for Akela. Of more than two hundred Red Dogs, not one got away.

9 THE SPRING RUNNING

Mowgli was now 17 years old. Living in the Jungle had made him strong and hard. He could swing by one hand from a branch for a long time. He could catch a running deer and throw it on its side. The Jungle People had come to fear him as much as they loved him.

Winter had ended. Mowgli and Bagheera were resting in the sunshine.

"Spring is here," said Bagheera. "Even the leaves seem to know it."

"Bagheera," Mowgli said in a cross voice, "stop rolling on your back like a kitten."

"But spring is here," said Bagheera. But he rolled over and sat up.

In a tree a little yellow bird started singing its spring song.

"Do you hear that, Mowgli?" Bagheera asked. "The bird knows what time of year it is. Now I, too, must remember my song." And Bagheera began singing to himself.

Mowgli looked around him. "Why are you singing? There is no game near by that I can see."

"Are both your ears stopped up, Little

Brother?" asked Bagheera. "That was no hunting song. That was the song I'll sing to my mate."

"Oh, now I remember," Mowgli said. His voice grew angry. "In the spring, you and the others run away. I, Mowgli, am left alone. What happened last year when I sent you to bring back Hathi?"

"He came only two nights late," said Bagheera.

"He did not come as soon as I wanted," Mowgli cried. "No. He was running around the Jungle, roaring through his trunk. His trail was like the trail of three elephants. He was even dancing. I saw him do it. But he would not come to me."

"But it was spring," said Bagheera. "Go to sleep, Little Brother. You are tired."

Spring in India is full of wonder. The rain wakes up all the trees and flowers. There is a noise of growing you can almost hear. It is the sound of a warm, happy world.

Until this year, Mowgli had always loved the spring. He liked the warm air on his face. He liked the hot sun on his back. He would run for miles and miles every spring.

The Jungle People are always very happy in the spring. They do not hunt. They are with their mates all night and day. And the young go looking for mates of their own. This is what the spring singing is all about.

But this year, Mowgli felt bad. "My insides hurt," he said to himself. "I don't know what is happening to me. I have been cross to Bagheera, and others as well. I feel hot and cold at the same time. It might be that a run would make me feel better. I'll call my four wolf brothers. They are growing fat. A run will do them good, too."

He called, but not one of his brothers answered. All the Jungle People seemed to be singing—all but Mowgli. He was alone.

"Good hunting, Little Brother!" called Chil, the kite. He and his mate flew close to Mowgli's head. And then they went off together into the sky.

Two young wolves came by. They were looking for open ground in which to fight. It was only a spring fight. They were fighting over a mate. Mowgli knew better than to try to stop a spring fight. It is part of the Jungle Law. But this year, everything seemed to make him angry. He caught the young wolves by the necks. With a quick shake of their backs, they pushed him away and were gone.

"I must be poisoned," Mowgli said. "They pushed me away as if I were a cub. And I feel as weak as a cub. I am poisoned. And soon the poison will kill me."

That night, Mowgli started to run. His running that night was more like flying. He went like the wind.

Late that night, Mowgli stopped running. "Well," he said to himself, "I can still run a little. It may be that the poison is not going to kill me. What is that over there?" He looked up the river.

"There are houses by the river," he said. "I wonder if this Man Pack is any better than the one I knew. I think I'll have a look."

Three or four dogs barked as he came close to the houses. The door of one of the houses opened. A woman looked out into the night. Inside the house, a child cried. The woman called, "Go back to sleep. Everything is all right."

Mowgli began to shake all over. He knew that voice well. "Messua! Oh, Messua!" he cried out. He was surprised that he remembered man talk.

"Who calls?" asked Messua.

"Don't you remember me," Mowgli asked, stepping into the light.

Messua looked up into his face. She took hold of his hands. "My son, is it you? But you are so tall and strong! Where is the boy I knew?"

Messua was getting old. Her hair was turning gray. But her eyes and her voice were still young.

"Come in, my son. Come in," she said, pulling him by the arm. "I am so happy to see you."

"I did not know you were here," Mowgli said.

"After I went to Khanhiwara," Messua said, "I met a man. He brought me here to make our home. Now we have a child. If you are my son, he is your brother. Come. Hold your brother in your arms."

She held a child out to Mowgli. He was only two years old. At first the child was afraid. But then he laughed in Mowgli's arms.

Messua said, "Let me make a fire. You shall have some warm milk."

Messua patted Mowgli's arm. "My son," she said, "you have become very good-looking." Laughing, she turned to the child. "See what a good-looking brother you have," she said. The little boy laughed back at her. Mowgli laughed too, though he did not know why.

The warm milk after his long run made Mowgli fall asleep. He was asleep all night and all the next day. When he got up, he was very hungry. Messua made dinner. Then they sat and talked.

After a while, there was a noise at the front door. A big gray paw pushed its way under the door. It was Gray Brother.

"You would not come when I called," Mowgli said to Gray Brother. "Now you can wait."

"Please," said Messua, "don't let him in." There was fear in her voice.

Mowgli said, "But Messua, he is your friend. He watched over you on your way to Khanhiwara." Then Mowgli smiled. "Mother," he said, "I must go."

Messua held out her hand. "Come back again," she said. "Look! Even the child cries because you are going away. We love you. Night or day, this door is never shut to you."

"I will come back," said Mowgli. Then he went outside to Gray Brother.

As soon as he saw Mowgli, Gray Brother jumped up. "What were you doing with the Man Pack?" he asked.

Mowgli was about to answer when he saw a girl in a white dress. She was young and very beautiful. She was coming down the trail toward

Mowgli. But when she saw him, she cried out and ran away. Mowgli stood and watched her until she was gone.

Mowgli turned back to Gray Brother. "Why did you not come when I called you? Don't you follow me any more?"

"We follow you," Gray Brother said. "We always follow you. But it is spring. You know how we are in the spring."

"Would you follow me to the Man Pack?" Mowgli asked.

"I followed you to the Man Pack once," Gray Brother answered. "Who was it that woke you when you were sleeping in the fields?"

"Yes," Mowgli said. "I remember. But would you follow me to the Man Pack again?"

"Did I not come to the Man Pack just now?" Gray Brother said. "Your trail is my trail. Your kill is my kill. And your death fight is my death fight. I speak for my three brothers as well."

"Then go tell my friends to meet me at the Council Rock," said Mowgli. "I must say good-by to them."

Gray Brother ran through the Jungle. "Mowgli goes back to the Man Pack!" he cried. "Come to the Council Rock!"

At any other time, all the Jungle would have answered. But it was spring. The happy Jungle

People called back, "He will come home again. He will come back to the Jungle. Come sing with us, Gray Brother."

At the Council Rock, Mowgli found only Baloo, Kaa, and his four brothers. When he saw them, Mowgli threw himself down on the ground. He hid his face in his hands.

"Cry your cry," Kaa said. "We be of one blood, you and I, man and snake together."

"I don't know what is happening to me," said Mowgli. "My bones are like water."

"What need is there of talk?" asked old Baloo. "As Akela once said, Mowgli will drive Mowgli back to the Man Pack."

"The Jungle is not throwing me out?" asked Mowgli.

"No, Little Frog," said Baloo. "I taught you the Law. Listen to me now. You must make your home with your own people. You will find a mate. Then you will have cubs of your own. But you are still Master of the Jungle. The Jungle People love you."

His words were cut short by a roar. Bagheera, as light and strong as ever, ran up to the Council Rock. He rubbed his head on Mowgli's leg. "You must make your own trail, Little Brother," he said. "But remember, Bagheera loves you." Then he ran back toward the Jungle. At the foot of the hill, he stopped. "Good hunting on the new trail!" he called. "Master of the Jungle, remember, Bagheera loves you."

"You must go," Baloo said. "But first, come to me." Baloo put his front legs around Mowgli and held him close.

Mowgli could not stop crying. Kaa put his head close to Mowgli's ear. "It is hard to climb out of an old skin," he said. "But it must be done. You will be happy with your own people."

"The stars begin to shine," said Gray Brother. He pulled at Mowgli's hand. "I wonder where we will sleep this night? From now on, we follow new trails."